Tortoise and Hare's Amazing Race

by Marianne Berkes   illustrated by Cathy Morrison

Henry Hare was always bragging. "I can run faster than anybody, especially Tess Tortoise. How does she ever get anywhere?"

"I plan ahead and stay on track," said Tess. "That's very wise," commented Oliver Owl.

Henry sprinted as fast as he could to the base of a hill. "Look at me, everyone!" boasted Henry, "I could make it all the way to the top before Tess even gets this far."

"How far is it to the top of the hill?" asked Tess.

"1,760 yards," hooted Oliver.

"That's a whole mile!" croaked Freddy Frog.

Henry came dashing back. "Or 5,280 feet. Tess could never do it!"

"Never say never," said Tess, annoyed by Henry's bragging.

"Ha! That's ridiculous! Tomorrow morning, I'll race Tess to the top to prove it. Set the time, Oliver, and I'll be there. Right now, I've got to run." Henry was gone in a flash.

Oliver knew Tess was very slow. He suggested Sally Squirrel accept the challenge instead.

"No, I need to do this," said Tess. "Sally can be the judge and meet me at the finish line."

Oliver mapped out the course and set the starting time for six a.m.

Many forest animals came to see the amazing race. Henry and Tess stood at the starting line.

"Ready, set, go!" hooted Oliver. The crowd began to cheer.

Henry got way ahead of Tess. At one-eighth of a mile, he sprinted off the track to chase some butterflies in the meadow. "I even have time to play," decided Henry.

1/8 mile

When Henry grew tired of chasing butterflies, he went back to the track. He was surprised to see Tess. "She may have gotten this far, but I'll get way ahead of her again in no time." Henry took off as fast as he could.

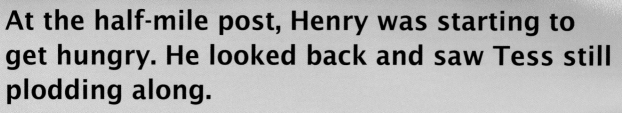

At the half-mile post, Henry was starting to get hungry. He looked back and saw Tess still plodding along.

"Time for some lunch," said Henry. He dashed off the track to find lettuce and carrots at a nearby farm.

Tess saw Henry go off the track as she kept on, saying to herself: "Even though I am behind, I have the finish line in mind."

When Henry came back, satisfied from a meal of lettuce and carrots, he saw that Tess was closing the gap.

"I'll just get way ahead of her again," said Henry. He sprinted as fast as he could to the three-quarter mile post.

When Henry got there, he was exhausted. He checked his GPS. Henry had run 3,960 feet on the track, in the hot sun. "One lucky thing for Tess," he thought, "is that she carries her house with her and can get shade whenever she wants."

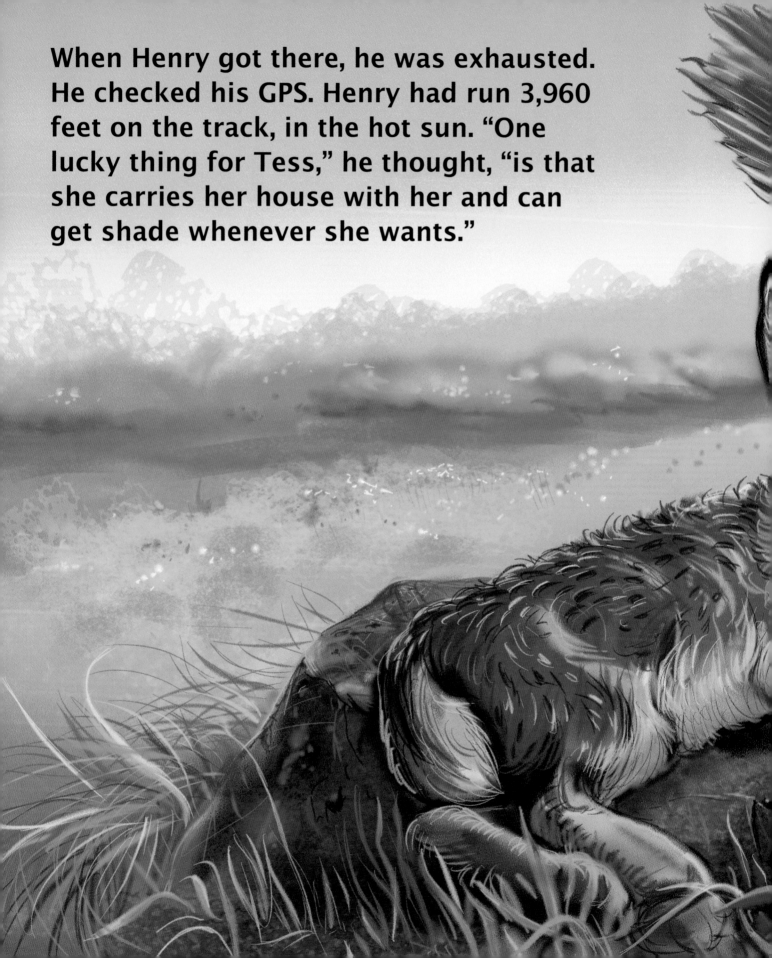

Feeling very tired and still full from his big meal, Henry stretched himself out under a shady tree. "I'm still ahead of her," he said drowsily. "Time for a nap!"

Tess kept going and eventually passed Henry as he snored and dreamed of victory.

It was eight p.m. when Tess heard the friendly sounds of animals cheering her on as she approached the finish line. Henry woke up and realized the cheers were not for him. He had slept way too long. Henry dashed frantically back on the track, but his leap was too late. The determined tortoise had walked 5,280 feet up the hill. Henry admitted in disgrace that slow and steady won the race!

For Creative Minds

Units of Measurement

A mile is a unit of measurement. Miles measure length or distance. Other, smaller units of measurement also measure length or distance.

An **inch** is a small unit of measurement. On most adults, an inch is about the length of the last joint of the thumb.

↓

A **foot** is twelve inches long. This is about the length of an adult's forearm (from elbow to wrist).

↓

A **yard** is three feet long. A tall adult can be two yards tall.

↓

A mile is 5,280 feet long, or 1,760 yards long. That is as long as about 960 people lying down in a line, feet to head.

foot = 12 inches
yard = 3 feet = 36 inches
eighth mile = 220 yards = 660 feet
quarter mile = 440 yards = 1,320 feet
half mile = 880 yards = 2,640 feet
mile = 1,760 yards = 5,280 feet

Measure It!

Small units of measurement, like inches or feet, are best for measuring small objects or distances. Large units of measurement, like miles, are best for measuring large distances.

Choose whether you would measure the following in inches, feet, or miles. Answers are below.

1. distance between your elbow and your shoulder
2. distance from your home to your school
3. length of a basketball court
4. height of a house
5. length of your foot
6. distance from the earth to the moon
7. height of a toy doll
8. length of a car
9. distance between two cities
10. height from the floor to the seat of a chair
11. length of your hair
12. distance from the capitol of a state to Washington DC.
13. length of a hallway
14. length of your big toe
15. length of a highway from one side of your state to the other

There are different tools you can use to measure things. Most **rulers** can measure things up to a foot long. Rulers are marked in inches. **Yardsticks** can measure things up to 1 yard long. Yardsticks are marked in inches and feet. **Tape measures** come in different sizes, often between 10 and 25 feet long. Tape measures are marked in inches and feet.

Think about it: What measurement tool works best for small lengths? Which are easier for measuring large lengths? To measure the length of a room, would you rather use a ruler or a tape measure? Would you use a ruler or a yardstick to measure the width of a hare's paw? Why?

Answers: 1—inches. 2—miles. 3—feet. 4—feet. 5—inches. 6—miles. 7—inches. 8—feet. 9—miles. 10—inches. 11—inches. 12—miles. 13—feet. 14—inches. 15—miles

Inches

Equal to, Greater than, Less than

When two values are the same, you can use the "equal" sign to show their relationship.

$$1 \text{ foot} = 12 \text{ inches}$$

When one value is larger than another, you can use the "greater than" sign to show their relationship.

$$1 \text{ yard} > 1 \text{ foot}$$

When one value is smaller than another, you can use the "less than" sign to show their relationship.

$$1 \text{ inch} < 1 \text{ foot}$$

An easy way to remember the "greater than" and "less than" signs is to think of it as an alligator's mouth. The alligator wants to eat the biggest meal possible, so the open end always faces the larger value.

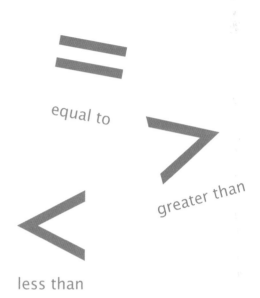

equal to

greater than

less than

Use the "equal to," "greater than," or "less than" sign to describe the relationships between the following distances. Answers are below.

A 1 mile __?__ 3,000 feet

B 3 feet __?__ 1 yard

C 6 inches __?__ 1 foot

D 5,280 feet __?__ 1 mile

E 1 foot __?__ 18 inches

F 2 feet __?__ 1 yard

G 1 inch __?__ 1 mile

H 1,760 yards __?__ 1 mile

I 1 yard __?__ 36 inches

Answers: A >, B =, C <, D =, E <, F <. G<, H =, I =

Animals of All Sizes

Animals come in all shapes and sizes. Put the animals below in order from largest to smallest to unscramble the word for a large unit of measurement.

I   Owls are birds. They hunt at night and rest during the day (nocturnal). Owls are meat-eaters (carnivores) that catch and eat smaller animals for food. Great horned owls are some of the most common owls in North America. They grow to 25 inches tall.

M   Tortoises are reptiles. Tortoises live on land and have a thick, hard shell to protect them from predators. Most tortoises eat only plants (herbivores). There are many kinds of tortoises. The largest, the Galapagos tortoise, is 5 feet long.

S   Frogs are amphibians. When frogs hatch, they live in the water. As they grow, they develop legs and lungs to move out of the water onto land. Frogs are carnivores. The largest frog in North America, the American bullfrog, is 6 inches long.

L   Hares are mammals related to rabbits. One of the most common hares in North America is the black-tailed jackrabbit. Like other hares, they have long, powerful back legs that they use to kick and jump. Black-tailed jackrabbits are herbivores. They grow up to 2 feet (24 inches) tall.

E   Squirrels are mammals in the rodent family. Like other rodents, they have front teeth that never stop growing. Squirrels gnaw to keep their teeth from getting too big. The American red squirrel is an herbivore and eats only conifer seeds. Including their tails, American red squirrels grow to 12 inches long.

Answer: MILES

For my granddaughter, Elisabeth, who also likes to write stories and loves music and math. Love—MB
To Marianne Berkes, an awesome writer and friend!—CM
Thanks to Carla Woodard, 3rd and 4th grade teacher in Durham, NC, for reviewing the accuracy of the information in this book.

Library of Congress Cataloging-in-Publication Data

Berkes, Marianne Collins.
  Tortoise and Hare's amazing race / by Marianne Berkes ; illustrated by Cathy Morrison.
    pages cm
  Summary: Fractions and distance measurements mark the progress of Henry Hare and Tess Tortoise as they race each other one mile up a hill.
  ISBN 978-1-62855-635-3 (English hardcover) -- ISBN 978-1-62855-640-7 (English pbk.) -- ISBN 978-1-62855-650-6 (English downloadable ebook) -- ISBN 978-1-62855-660-5 (English interactive dual-language ebook) -- ISBN 978-1-62855-645-2 (Spanish pbk.) -- ISBN 978-1-62855-655-1 (Spanish downloadable ebook) -- ISBN 978-1-62855-665-0 (Spanish interactive dual-language ebook) [1. Measurement--Fiction. 2. Turtles--Fiction. 3. Hares--Fiction. 4. Racing--Fiction.] I. Morrison, Cathy, illustrator. II. Title.
  PZ7.B45258To 2015
  [E]--dc23
                                        2015009002

Translated into Spanish by Rosalyna Toth in collaboration with Federico Kaiser: *La asombrosa carrera entre la tortuga y la liebre*

Lexile® Level: AD 610L
key phrases for educators: distance measurements, fables/folktales, fractions, measurements, anthropomorphic, counting

Manufactured in China, June 2015
This product conforms to CPSIA 2008
First Printing

Arbordale Publishing
Mt. Pleasant, SC 29464
www.ArbordalePublishing.com